THE ART

Shadowscapes
Tarot

MAJOR ARCANA

STEPHANIE PUI-MUN LAW

Llewellyn Publications

Woodbury, Minnesota

Reprint Edition
First Printing, 2017
This book was originally published by Shadowscapes Inc. www.shadowscapes.com.

Cover art ©2003–2009 by Stephanie Pui-Mun Law
Cover design by Lisa Novak

Llewellyn Publications is a registered trademark of Llewellyn Worldwide Ltd.

Library of Congress Cataloging-in-Publication Data
Names: Law, Stephanie Pui-Mun.
Title: The art of shadowscapes tarot / Stephanie Pui-Mun Law.
Description: First edition. | Woodbury : Llewellyn Worldwide, Ltd, 2017.
Identifiers: LCCN 2016029325 | ISBN 9780738751290
Subjects: LCSH: Tarot.
Classification: LCC BF1879.T2 L385 2017 | DDC 133.3/2424--dc23 LC record
available at https://lccn.loc.gov/2016029325

Llewellyn Worldwide Ltd. does not participate in, endorse, or have any authority or responsibility concerning private business transactions between our authors and the public.

All mail addressed to the author is forwarded but the publisher cannot, unless specifically instructed by the author, give out an address or phone number.

Any Internet references contained in this work are current at publication time, but the publisher cannot guarantee that a specific location will continue to be maintained. Please refer to the publisher's website for links to authors' websites and other sources.

Llewellyn Publications
A Division of Llewellyn Worldwide Ltd.
2143 Wooddale Drive
Woodbury, MN 55125-2989
www.llewellyn.com

Printed in the United States of America

Introduction

In an attempt to get me to stop using her house as my extra storage space, my mother settled two large boxes of "Old Stuff" into my trunk the last time I was visiting. She said it was a box of my love letters that she wasn't going to toss (I could have the honors myself). I suspect she was being facetious.

After driving about with said "Old Stuff" for a week and having it rattle complaints each time I took a sharp turn or raced through a yellow traffic light, I finally got around to sifting through it all as I was rummaging around for lost art supplies.

No love letters. But I was surprised to come across something that I had thought long discarded: some old tarot cards I had started, once upon a time. There was no date on these relics, but I think it must have been around 1988. I have a vague recollection of learning about this thing called the tarot in junior high and being fascinated by it. I was determined to make my own deck, though apparently I never got further than seven cards and one sketch. Extended attention span to complete such a lengthy project at that age was a bit much to ask for.

Holding these drawings from two decades prior in my hand brought a wave of nostalgia. As I stared at them, I was amazed to discover similarities in the crude drawings to the finished product of more recent years. Even though I had forgotten about this first attempt, in the intervening span of time my mind had remained remarkably consistent in its aesthetic goals and the treatment of concepts.

I remember hunching over at my desk, creating these and knowing (without being able to really put it to words at that time) that what really reeled me in was the chance to depict my own personal mythology while drawing from a rich language of symbolism and archetypes. It was what still reeled me in and led me down the path to complete the deck earlier this year.

And I do feel that "path" has been almost a literal description for the project, winding out from the Fool stepping off from her precipice, to the World, and then beyond into the minor arcana. It has been an extended mental exercise in meditation as I started each image, internalized it, and searched for the personal connections to create my own meaning and mode of expression for the concepts, emotions, or personae. It has been about finding my own links in order to define this, my personal mythos.

And thus, secondary to being simply a collection of the Shadowscapes Tarot artwork, this book is meant to share the thoughts and inspirations from which each piece stemmed. I find the sketches leading up to a painting to sometimes tell stories of their own. I invite you to have a peek into my sketchbooks to witness some of the processes of how these paintings came into being, along with some of the accompanying concepts, sketches, and thoughts.

Stephanie Pui-Mun Law

April 19, 2009

Table of Contents

Fool 4

Magician 8

High Priestess 12

Empress 16

Emperor 20

Hierophant 24

Lovers 28

Chariot 32

Strength 36

Hermit 40

Wheel of Fortune 44

Justice 48

Hanged Man 52

Death 56

Temperance 60

Devil 64

Tower 68

Star 72

Moon 76

Sun 80

Judgment 84

World 88

Cycles 92

Fool

It begins with a whispered voice. The serpentine song threads through her days and her thoughts. It beckons: Come … come … come … *"Where?"* she asks, curious, but there is no response.

She ignores the summons, until one day that siren song unexpectedly explodes and fills her to the brim. Its pulse is undeniable. *"Where?"* she asks again, and this time the steady beat of her heart is the response.

The Fool has come a long way, traveled from far beyond to come to this pinnacle that rises up upon the edge of the world; and yet her journey is just about to begin. She senses this with instinctive perceptions as she rises up upon her toes, caught up in the breathless embrace of the wind in the moment before the plunge. Her heart pounds and flutters in her chest with the force of a hundred beating wings, struggling to break free of the cage of her being; until she feels she must be sprouting wings from her shoulders to glide forth from that place, transformed.

Wait! Don't! cries a thin trailing voice from within. *Caution! Fear!* it rails. *Hold back!*

Unheeding, she steps forward, and …

MEANING

She stands on the edge of a very sheer precipice, with only the ribbons and the doves bearing her up if she chooses to leap. The fox takes this in. He watches. He is the embodiment of cleverness, but being clever does not preclude being a fool of a different sort. He can't comprehend the leap of faith that she is about to take. So who's the fool, she for stepping out into the unknown in what seems a complete lack of logic, or the fox for being too firmly rooted in the belief of the reality of intellectual thought?

The Fool is a symbol for new beginnings and adventures, pleasure and passion. She rushes ahead, thoughtless and rash, doing before thinking, obeying instincts. Like the Fool, you may stand upon the precipice gazing out into the unknown. The endless expanse of blue nothing is all that fills the space between that high up aerie and the ground that is so very far away. There is either an oblivious foolishness to the terrible plunge you may experience or else a wild spirit of adventure and great faith and knowledge in that which can and will bear you up and guide through the times to come. There are unlimited possibilities opening up for the seeker.

Fool

I felt a personal connection to this
card as I started out.
Perhaps it was
simply because it
was the first one, but it seemed fitting
that it was a card emblematic of beginnings.
It was a mirror to a journey I was embarking on.

Rising up on tiptoe, leaning out over an abyss.
Nothing but the invisible arms of the wind
to hold back from a fall, and these fragile
little birds with their ribbons.

Mere illusions of safety?

Physically there is nothing to stop her from tumbling.

6/13/04

By setting obviously
inadequate physical
barriers to her fall, I hoped
to create the implication
that perhaps there is the
unseen aspect to that
which will bear her up
on this journey that
she insists on throwing
herself headlong into.

the physical
heart-body

the
spirit
enclosed
in a rose

Monkey thoughts:
Representatives of the primal form of
humanity before conscious thoughts,
conscience, and concepts of wisdom or
foolery.

the embodiment
of the soul
a butterfly

A trip to the
San Diego Zoo to
spy on & sketch the
macaques. Perched in
a row on the limb,
like a flock of
strange birds

More monkey thoughts:

"See no evil, hear no evil, speak no evil"
a kind of oblivious innocence. Close
it all out with a blank mind!

By shutting out the perils of
the world, can one plow an
uninfluenced path?

Or is that just folly?

I chose to make my fool
female vs. the more standard
male as a signifier of my
own connection to her,
as we began our
journey in tandem.

Magician

The Fool drifts past as a seed in the wind, as a twirling feather, as a crystal mote of condensation, and she sees the Magician. She watches the boy who is initiated to the mysteries of the elements. He is taught and masters: conjurings, summonings, bindings.

One day she cannot resist, and she trails fingers of wind across his eyes and he opens them with a start, seeing for a moment. *"Who are you?"* he demands, but oh so quickly the spirit transforms into a stag and bounds away.

He chases into the woods. Always the stag is just out of reach. His bare feet press into the earth. The air rushes through his hair. The sun beats upon his shoulders. The tantalizing flash of white from the stag darting through the verdure taunts him unbearably until suddenly …

It is gone, and he is alone.

Upon a rock he sees the gifts that have been left for him. The relics of the elements glint in the sunlight, and as his hands close upon the offerings, a smile touches his lips at the power that surges through them.

MEANING

Originality, creativity, skill, willpower, self-confidence, dexterity, and slight of hand. It is about grasping the unseen around you and harnessing it to become reality. Drawing forth the ineffable into the material realm of existence. This Magician draws upon relics representative of the elements: Fire in his lantern, the voice of the sea in the shell, a breath of wind in the raven's feather, and earth from the leaves. He knows what he wants, and he knows he can make it happen with conscious exertion of his will and his knowledge of how to manipulate the world.

Magician
FROM THE SKETCHBOOK

He started off with a different pose, but it felt too imposing. Domination rather than creation. Not what he is meant to be; that would be encroaching upon the Emperor. The Magician's realm is more to channel power into physical manifestation, directing the nebulous with his desires.

But his general design appealed, and so I kept most of it while rearranging the pose. It was modified to a stance that was not so aggressive and looming face-on. Turned to the side to deflect some of the aggression. Turned inward for the sake of focus of the will and to draw his powerful spirit to be molded in the space between his hands.

The relics, the essences of which later make their reappearance in the minor arcana:

A flame caught in lantern. The blazing ember of a fire elemental. The flicker of fireflies blinking on a summer night.

A handful of leaves, green and flowing with living sap. The bounty of the earth that can be spun into being by such ephemeral things as light and air. In her way, Nature is a Magician.

The crashing sea captured in the curl of a seashell.

On Roses and Lilies:

…I am haunted by numberless
  islands, and many a Danaan shore,
Where Time would surely forget us,
  and Sorrow come near us no more;
Soon far from the rose and the lily,
  and fret of the flames would we be,
Were we only white birds, my beloved,
  buoyed out on the foam of the sea!

  —W. B. Yeats, "The White Birds"

Lilies of death-pale hope, roses of passionate dream.

  —W. B. Yeats, "The Travail of Passion"

The sylphs of the sky. They tumble like careless acrobats in the wind, stretching wings out to touch the corners of the heavens.

High Priestess

The High Priestess turns her face to the sky. She basks in the radiance the stars cast upon her upturned cheeks. She soaks in that tremulous incandescent light, feeling it glow within her mind, opening corridors and dancing in filigree patterns. The stars chant:

We were here when the mountains were young

and the sea was only a dream

we've seen the hills bloom with countless millions of seasons

we've watched the clouds paint their visions

in a slow language across the centuries

let us speak.

At the light brush of a moth's wing across her palm, she turns her gaze to it.

"Take this as a present to your mistress," she says. She plucks the filigree orb of light from the air and holds it out to the emissary of the Moth Queen. "I know my sister appreciates tales. Tell her that this holds the stories of the stars."

The little orb pulses with a fiery heartbeat, and the moth flutters as if to acknowledge.

MEANING

Wisdom, knowledge, learning, intuition, purity, virtue. The High Priestess lifts her arms out, and in that gesture, her very body becomes the living symbol of a chalice. The owl is a keeper of knowledge, and he bears a key to unlock mysteries. The pomegranate is an icon of Persephone, who tasted the seeds and thus tied herself to Hades—it is a fruit of fertility and death; and the moons embroidered upon her garments wax and wane. The new crescent and gibbous moon that create the full cycle, embraced in one.

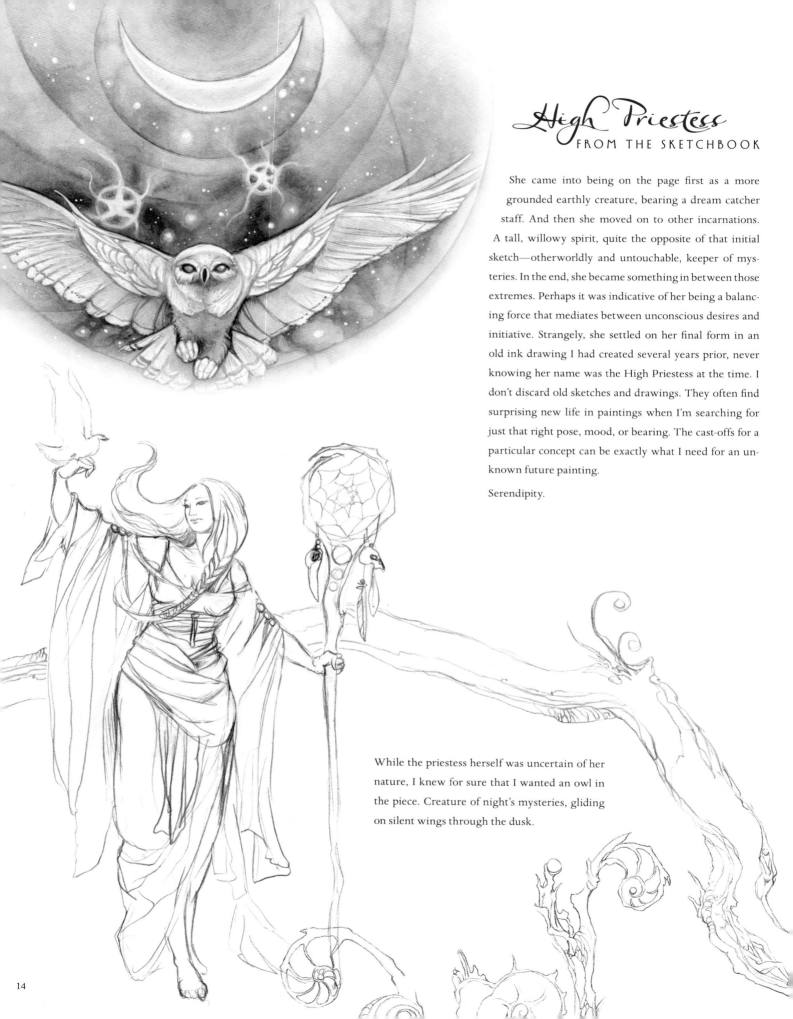

High Priestess
FROM THE SKETCHBOOK

She came into being on the page first as a more grounded earthly creature, bearing a dream catcher staff. And then she moved on to other incarnations. A tall, willowy spirit, quite the opposite of that initial sketch—otherworldly and untouchable, keeper of mysteries. In the end, she became something in between those extremes. Perhaps it was indicative of her being a balancing force that mediates between unconscious desires and initiative. Strangely, she settled on her final form in an old ink drawing I had created several years prior, never knowing her name was the High Priestess at the time. I don't discard old sketches and drawings. They often find surprising new life in paintings when I'm searching for just that right pose, mood, or bearing. The cast-offs for a particular concept can be exactly what I need for an unknown future painting.

Serendipity.

While the priestess herself was uncertain of her nature, I knew for sure that I wanted an owl in the piece. Creature of night's mysteries, gliding on silent wings through the dusk.

On Dream Catchers:

There is a Native American legend in which an Elder had a vision. He was instructed by Iktomi, the great trickster and teacher of wisdom, in the form of a spider, of the cycles of life. As Iktomi spoke, he spun a web across the Elder's willow hoops, and from this created a dream catcher web. The elder passed on his vision to his people.

Dream catchers are hung above one's bed or in the home to sift dreams and visions. Good dreams flow through the hole in the center, while bad dreams are captured in the webbing to be burned off by the first touch of dawn's rays.

15

Empress

"Lady-Mother!" call the wandering souls. "We bring you gifts!" They fly near the Empress, dancing in the sky. They paint synchronized kaleidescope choreographies for her pleasure, and she smiles as she takes them in. Her mind and her thoughts are the conductor to this visual symphony.

Gently, they lay a crown woven of the first buds of spring across her brow. "Jasmine and Lily of the Valley have graciously donated their first buds for your coronet," the spirits sigh.

"The Apple Tree Man has gifted you with his fruit, and the Lady of the Fields her grains." These they lay in her basket.

With a sudden flourish, the spirits whirl together, then spin off in an explosion of light and music. "Farewell, dear Lady!" they call.

MEANING

Creativity, generosity, patience, love. The Empress is about abundance, experiencing the senses, and embracing the natural. She is a Creator. She is the Mother—fertile and nurturing. Clasped to her body like a child, she holds a basket of the earth's bounty: fruits and sheaves of wheat and glorious flowers. She is the primal essence and embodiment of Life, and is deeply tied to nature; she is crowned in ivy and clasped in garments the colors of the world around her.

Empress
FROM THE SKETCHBOOK

Fertility, abundance, and reveling in all of Creation. These were the key concepts I wanted to encompass in the Empress. The wild jumble of roses and the profusion of butterflies were meant to overwhelm the senses with riotous color, movement, and scent. Her gown curls around her like the silken petals of a rose, adding the sensual nature of touch to that mixture. (Incidentally, the color of those blooms and her garments is one that I have never been able to reproduce since; that exact order of layered colors and concentration of pigment which resulted in those tones eludes me, much to my frustration. Despite using the same watercolor set of twenty-four pigments for countless paintings since she came into being, she is unique.)

On Pomegranates:

An emblem of fruitfulness.

Speculated by some to be the forbidden fruit of Eden.

Persephone: Her story goes that she was the daughter of ancient Greek goddess Demeter (of Harvest). One day, Hades glimpsed Persephone alone in a field and was struck by her beauty. He kidnapped her and brought her into the darkness of the underworld to be his bride. There, Persephone was trapped, longing for the sun, refusing to eat anything until a bright pomegranate was brought to her. The ruby red seed sparked a longing within her, and so she ate four seeds, not knowing that the Fates decreed that anyone who consumed food in the underworld must stay there. As a result, she was forced to remain with Hades for four months of the year.

Despite that multitude of inspiration, the pomegranate born by that little bird in the initial sketch did not make its way into the final piece. Instead it found its home with the High Priestess.

tarot: the empress
7/13/04

19

Emperor

The Emperor remembers...

He remembers when once there was another man. Was it his father? A mentor? Or was it a vanquished king? His mind arcs back, grasping. Once there was another, and he relinquished the dragon orb.

He remembers his own fascination with the orb upon first laying eyes on it, and as he touched it the strength of the creature within surged through his arms and possessed his senses. "You are now the lord of these mortal realms." Was it the other who had said that? Or was it the dragon? He was now the dragon!

"Yessss," he said, and knew it was so.

MEANING

Creating order out of chaos, authority, leadership, strength, establishing law and order. The carvings on the wall bear the symbols of the domain, and of dominion. The eagle ascends above mountains and sea, night and day, ruling over all. The earthly creatures bow to that mastery. But even though the imagery of the carvings may be magnificent, still a wall is a man-made edifice; man's measure and means of controlling the wildness of the world by attempting to carve it into unchanging stone. Man's desire to control and etch out and write the story of his own destiny. The Emperor is a man rooted in his ways and views and regimens, but confident that this is the right and way of things; structure.

Emperor
FROM THE SKETCHBOOK

As opposed to the Empress, with her endless skies and the chaos of the wide open, I knew the Emperor would want to be surrounded by man-made walls. Edifices that would reinforce the supremacy and control that the conscious will and exercise of power can enforce upon one's surroundings.

The sigil on the wall was to be the record of his dominions. But what to depict?

A dragon? For the Chinese, it has long been a symbol of male energies, of the civilization triumphing over baser natural instincts. Though it has the physical form of a beast, it represents the melding of the best qualities of each creature it borrows from, tied together by the highest mental order—the human mind.

A lion? King of the beasts, with tawny mane like the sun itself and mighty roar.

Or perhaps an eagle! Soaring at the pinnacle. The creatures of the earth kneel under the shadow of the great bird's outspread wings, as well as the swirling stars and the blazing sun; all etched into the frieze that the Emperor stands before.

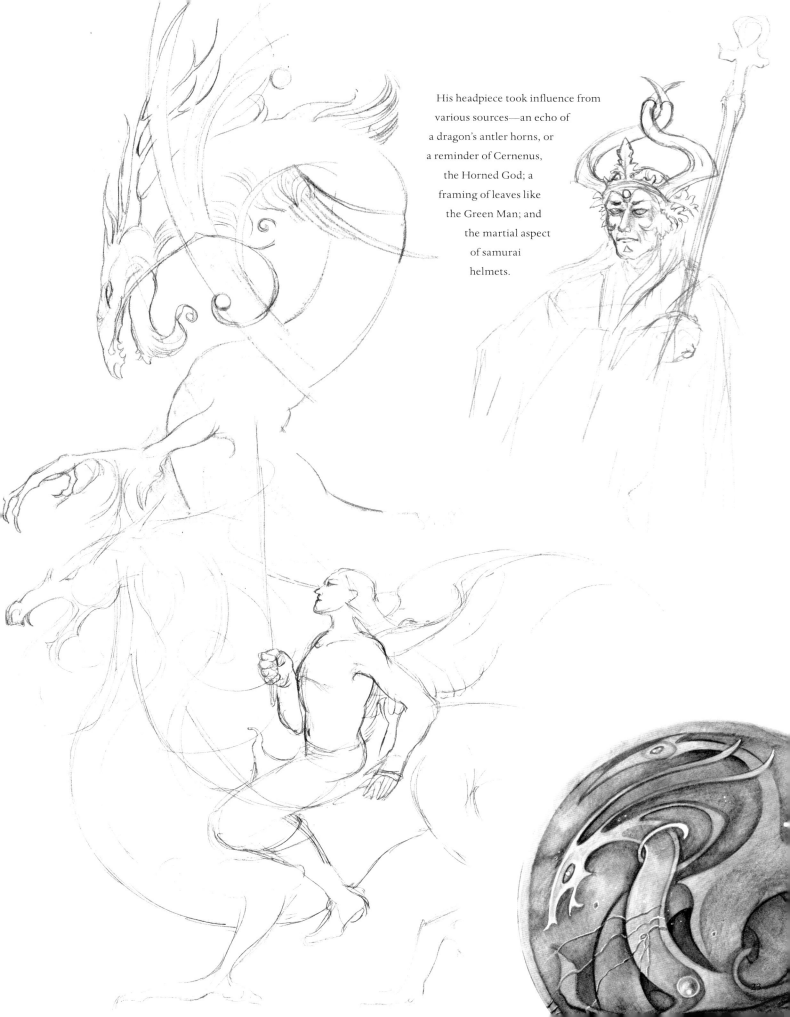

His headpiece took influence from
various sources—an echo of
a dragon's antler horns, or
a reminder of Cernenus,
the Horned God; a
framing of leaves like
the Green Man; and
the martial aspect
of samurai
helmets.

Hierophant

"I would like a story," says the salamander to the Hierophant.

"And what would you like to hear, little one?" The words come slowly. Each syllable seems to be drawn from deep within, pulled up from an individual rootlet. The salamander is used to it and patient.

"I want to hear how I may fly. I was content. And then one day friend Caterpillar said he was sleepy. He slept for a long time until I nearly forgot him. Until … yesterday a moth came to laugh at me. He laughed with Caterpillar's laugh, and with Caterpillar's voice he said he had had a dream of wings."

"Ah." The sonorous exhalation seems to go on forever. "Ah, little one; I am sorry. Caterpillar has that blessing. He may sleep and dream of flight. He weaves a silken ritual around his body, and then comes the day when that vision transforms him. You …"

"I wish to dream of flight, too!" says Salamander, very seriously.

"You may dream of it," says his friend and teacher. "I will not be the one to deny you divinity. But just know that your own divinity shall be attained along a different path than Caterpillar's. Do not relinquish your dream, Salamander."

MEANING

The Hierophant's roots are deep reaching, entwined around secrets and traditions and the ages. He believes in ritual and ceremony, pursuing knowledge and deeper meaning, the rigidity of a belief system. He elucidates the spiritual and brings it to the earthly plane. He is calm and in possession of himself, and is the teacher who can help unravel mysteries.

2009

Hierophant
FROM THE SKETCHBOOK

I struggled with finding my connection to this card, until I turned away from looking at other depictions of the Hierophant. The dominant image of him portrayed as a pope and religious leader struck no resonance with me, and it was only when I closed my eyes to those outside influences and concentrated instead on the heart of this piece's meaning that I found my muse for the Hierophant and the pathway to create his visage.

The Hierophant is a being who believes in the hierarchical structure of the world, finding his identity within the dictates of the group. He is metaphorically ancient, steeped in rules and rituals and traditions, stolid and unbending in his adherence to these.

9/19/04

With that in mind, the image that quickly came to me was of an elder tree spirit; an ancient of the forest, his roots spread far and deep into the soil from which he sprung centuries ago, and every fiber of his being is the product of the nutrients and knowledge and mysteries that have been buried and steeped into the rich loam that he buries his feet into.

And though in his way he might see and know more than the more mobile creatures of the world might ever learn in their fleeting lives, he is limited by being rooted to his spot. He intimately knows the way the sun shines through his leaves on each of the 365 days of the year. He knows the taste of the wind through the changing seasons and can sing with each variety of bird that passes through his branches; but he is nevertheless bound.

holly (evergreen) &
ivy (memory) crown
Taliesin druids

spiral stonehenge tattoos
closed 3 eyes
angelic surd on his head

The Hierophant
9/19/04

Lovers

In one of the oldest tales, there is the choice: knowledge and fulfillment of worldly senses or the simplicity of an ever-present now.

To be drawn into an embrace, to seek that union that all souls ache for and desire, to know the oneness of passion and love, and to revel in it. Their eyes are open, but they gaze only at each other; oblivious to the sun that goes on turning above them and the gaze of the heavens. Neither gold and gem-encrusted crown of kings nor the grapevine and flower twined crown of peasants grace their brows, for the forces gathering around them make no such distinctions; indeed their own senses have no awareness of such either.

Take this seed, he says to her, placing an acorn in her palm. *Water it with the fount of your spirit and your intentions.*

And we shall see what grows of that, she replies.

MEANING

Union, balance, energy, flow, love, desire, passion, melding of heart and mind, forming a union or marriage. Though it can be romantic in nature, it is not necessarily so. The Lovers is also about determining values and struggling with choices—the innocence embodied in the turtledoves is a contrast to the shiny red apple in the embrace of the snake, one of the oldest symbols of temptation. Likewise the pure simplicity of the calla lily to the lush and sensual complexity of a rose.

Inspiration for this arose from a quick sketch done at the Musée Rodin in Paris the summer I painted the Lovers. From a rough sketch of a sculpture to the rough scribble in a sketchbook to be transmuted a third time by the twists of memory and the intentional changes of brainstorming; taking on its final alchemized form. The story of its coming about echoes the eternally changing story of love itself.

Their eyes are closed in the initial sketch ... with the heedless absorption in their senses and with one another; but in the final painting (a detail that is all but invisible at actual card size) their eyes are wide open as they gaze at one another.

They do not make their choices in blind fits of passion, but rather with foreknowledge and a willingness to see everything.

That was the challenge of this piece: to balance the depiction of the Lovers as that word implies, but also integrating the key element of choices and the weightiness of decisions.

Tarot - Lovers

- two Mourning doves inflight (soul)
- apples?
- sun emblem on him
  moon edging
- lilies - innocence
- acorn - potential
- heart?

6/28/04

braided brown and
white tree roots
at their feet

On Acorns and Oaks:

Etched into the wall in the background is a Celtic triskelion
(a symbol of the cycles of life, honor, and fortitude) woven
of acorns. From such humble little
seeds there is the potential to
sprout into towering giants of
the forest!

Chariot

She is Winged Victory, the goddess Nike, or Maeve. She comes sweeping from the skies, confident and sure of herself. She has summoned the unicorns of the sea out from the foamy depths. They serve her willingly, bowing as is ever in their nature to only purity of intent. The very ocean swells themselves are tamed beneath the enchanted wheels of her chariot. The glittering waves crash and roar with the strength of the sea, but as she guides her unicorns across the glistening track, the waves fall still before her and into a quiescent and shining mirror path.

This stillness in that which is in eternal motion stirs awareness in the denizens of the deeps. From underneath, the spirits of the ocean whisper to the sea god, and in a swirl of aquatic color, they dance to the surface to greet one whose willpower and mastery is so undeniable as to be capable of overcoming even the wild natural fury of the seas.

MEANING

Triumph over obstacles, achieving victory, focusing intent and will, establishing an identity, self-confidence, maintaining discipline, assuming the reins of power and authority and driving with the unwavering certainty in a cause.

Control must be exercised in a constantly changing environment that can and will throw up challenges; in the landscape of a world that is constantly shifting with the people and emotions and circumstances all around. Like the tenuous border where sea meets sky, a constant tension of push and pull of air against liquid is maintained, and to ride to victory one must be able to achieve the confidence and knowledge to walk upon that fragile surface.

Chariot
FROM THE SKETCHBOOK

Winged Victory, Nike sweeping down from the heavens!

The choice of setting for this piece upon the shifting water's surface was to tie the powers of heaven and earth into her grasp. The distant castle among the clouds and the surging life in the ocean below her meet in that thin film that constitutes water's surface. To be able to ride across that fragile surface with such reckless abandon must therefore imply great self-mastery, and a daunting control over one's surroundings and reality.

warriorqueen?

unicorn   griphon   phoenix or lion   sea turtles

4 animals for earth/air/fire/water?

crab holding up a sun like egyptian sun beetle

driving/running on water perhaps on backs of turtles w/arcane symbols on shells   Oct. 6, 2004

On Unicorns and Narwhals:

It is thought that perhaps the unicorn's origins in the sea stemmed from the half-glimpsed shapes sailors saw darting in the watery depths of narwhals with those inexplicable gleaming horns.

And, in fact, narwhal tusks were passed off by northern traders during medieval times to princes as being the magical fluting horn of a unicorn.

They were a precious treasure indeed, imbued with magical poison-cleansing properties.

On Crabs:

Interestingly, the Cancer constellation in the night sky has, through various civilizations, been identified as a crab, a scarab (in ancient Egypt), and a tortoise (Babylonia).

Strength

The lion roars, the earth trembles, and the clouds skitter nervously. The bamboo sways gently. The Chinese know the hidden strength of bamboo: so fragile and delicate seeming, but flexible and strong. It is a strength that does not need to shout of its power to the world, but sways and bows to the wind, then springs gracefully forward again with a melodious rustle of leaves.

He roars again, and a flock of birds jolt from their perches to take flight at the sound. The maiden steps forward. She is as willowy as the stalks of the bamboo grove she emerges from. Step by step, unafraid, she approaches the beast. This king of the wilds watches her, and she meets him eye to eye.

A third time his mighty challenge echoes to the skies in a claim of mastery and ownership and dominion to any who hear it. She smiles as she comes within arm's length, and at her touch, the great golden head bows.

MEANING

Courage, calm composure and patience, compassion, persuasion and soft control, tempered force. Managing impulses to control anger and force, rather than be manipulated by them. One must have faith in success, though it might not come at once, and it may not come very easy—the lion is fierce, and the fire he guards is a flame that burns. Strength must be tempered sometimes. Unshakable resolve is what will see one through to the desired end.

There are many kinds of strength: There is fierce and bestial power, brute force of tooth and claw, the fierce winged protectiveness called forth by a swan for her young. There is the steady strength of an oak springing from a tiny acorn, but growing, growing, growing into a mighty tree. There is the strength of bamboo, swaying and internalizing forces from around but not breaking.

On Lion, Swan, and Acorn:

The Lion is easily recognized for its strength; if nothing else for its physical size, the power that lies coiled in those sinewy muscles, and the claws that can rend and tear. But it is a one-sided manifestation of strength, encompassing only the physical.

Then there is the Swan. For all her beauty and the apparent softness of her physical presence with pristine and downy white feathers and elegantly curved neck, she is a fierce fighter as well. Threaten her young and those wings would beat a mighty gust of protection.

The Acorn possesses a passive strength. Like the drip of water slowly eroding away even the hardest rock, the acorn has that slow and patient strength that curls within the tiny seed, awaiting the right time; and then shooting up into the world to slowly grow, Grow, GROW into a mighty oak tree.

These different types of strength were what I wished to encapsulate in the maiden, who gently lays her hand across the brow and jaw of such a terrifying creature.

On Bamboo:

The sound of the wind sighing through the top of a bamboo grove is a peaceful susurrus, the perfect invitation for meditation. The Bamboo was the final type of strength I wanted this image to possess—that which yields but does not break. To let the wind sing through one's outer reaches and to sway with those gales in a dance; instead of fighting and snapping. It is the knowledge of when to let forces wash over and around oneself, and of how to do so while standing tall.

Hermit

He is the seeker who has turned his back to the noise and light and distractions of the world. In the city, the fragile light of the stars is drowned by the glare and the haze of life.

He takes his lantern. He was told by the wise woman that it was a bit of a captured star, and it knows its way home. The lonely beam of light pulls him clear of the valleys, and high above a glittering lake whose surface is a liquid mirror. His star lantern marks the path, and he does not know where he goes, but each step lights the next, and the next, and the next.

He climbs to a distant pinnacle that is clear of the smog of humanity, and as he retreats, the air attains a spicy fragrance. It is a purity he does not know he has missed until he breathes it for the first time, and then it is as if the body aches for and cannot live without that breath of life. Others have been here before him, but the steps are pristine and there is no indication of their passage. It is the nature of that place that to each who comes, they are the first and the only, and no other will tread there until the present visitor is forgotten.

It is a long journey, and during the course of the trek, his eyes finally become accustomed to the darkness of the wild. He leaves behind his memory of the city. The star in his lantern burns hot and bright, and her sisters in the heavens swirl in a joyous dance.

MEANING

Being introspective, seeking solitude and withdrawing from the world, giving or receiving guidance. The hermit is an inspirational friend and teacher, and his help can illuminate the secrets of one's own mind. That which was mysterious can be made clear with the proper light to shine upon the situation. The loons glide on silent wings across the horizon, elusive shadows in the night. They are symbols of peace and tranquility, and their eerily haunting call that echoes across waterways is laden with ancient wisdom. Loons are also respected for their knowledge of the sky, sea, and forest worlds, and were often seen in the headdresses of Indian chiefs.

Hermit
FROM THE SKETCHBOOK

On Nautilus Spirals:

Fossils embedded into the pillar that the Hermit climbs, an indication of its ancient nature. Particularly, nautilus shells—symbols of beauty and proportional perfection. The ever-widening chambers like his reaching mind and expanding consciousness.

Meditation from a high up perch

On Loons:

The first time I heard the cry of the loons and saw their dark shapes slip out across the water was with my husband's family at Lake Manatou. In the almost perfect silence of dawn and dusk, a line of phantom shadows would skim across the lake's mirror surface in the distance. Their strange call would betray their identity. It is no surprise that loons were seen as spirit creatures to the Indians. There is something otherworldly in the experience of encountering them. Like the faery creatures of other cultures, their choice of timing at dawn and dusk seem to mark the transition moments of the day; when doors to the otherworld are opened briefly and realities exist in a nebulous way.

On the Night Sky:

To glimpse the Milky Way in the night sky is a rare thing for most people, surrounded as we are by so much light pollution that turns the "black" of night into something more of a smoky gray with faint pinpricks of light twinkling through the haze. As such, to actually be able to see that clear pathway of distant stars and dust in the sky is a true indication of solitude. Far from the light of freeways with the ant-like progression of headlamps, and the collective glow of a thousand television sets burning sullenly through family room windows. Far from the noise that comes hand in hand with all that.

Tarot-hermit- 11/14/04

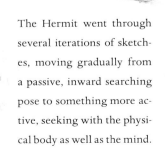

The Hermit went through several iterations of sketches, moving gradually from a passive, inward searching pose to something more active, seeking with the physical body as well as the mind.

Wheel of Fortune

Storybooks begin, "Once upon a time …" and then like a neatly wrapped package, they come to "The End."

But true tales have no beginning or end. They do not exist only when men say "Exist!" but are always there … reverberating through time in a weaving dance. We try to contain it with beginnings and ends, to put boundaries on everything simply because our own lives are bounded by birth and death. And thus we seek to lessen the power of that which is immortal. True tales have a power that reaches beyond.

The Fates weave the threads of life eternally, one tied to another. Snip this thread here. Weave it into the tapestry there. Slowly as the cloth rolls away the images emerge.

Night follows day in the cycle of the heavens. Year blooms with the first fresh buds of spring, to the sweltering profusion of long summer days, and the shower of leaves as autumn sets in, and then the long dormant wait and sleep of winter … and on it goes, and on.

It is an inexorable and timeless tale.

The walls and beauty that artisans create will one day fall, and new will rise up on those remains. And so do the individual fortunes of any one person, on a cycle that may last a day or two, or years on end. The Change will come.

MEANING

The Wheel of Fortune—Destiny, the weaving of life's threads coming together, fate, turning points, movement and change, patterns and cycles, an interconnected world. The knot work in the stained glass window is a single golden line that circles around the wheel as a continuous thread without start or finish. The rise and fall of the wheel as it turns is as the changes of life. If the world seems to be closing in and crushing hope with its weight, step back to see the bigger picture and the upturn that is soon to come.

The Wheel of Fortune started off in my mind as the female figure of Lady Luck. But after several iterations, I realized she was not working. I shifted the focus to the actual wheel.

What did it signify? The circular nature of fortune, the inevitable rise and fall (or conversely the fall and rise) of all things, and the interconnected web of reality. Fortune and growth in one area is balanced by entropy and decay in another quarter, all to cycle back and renew.

On the Fates:

Perhaps another incarnation of Fortune. They go by many names. To the ancient Greeks, they were the Moirae: Clotho (the maiden), Lachesis (the mother), and Atropos (the crone); spinning, measuring, and cutting the threads of life for all mortals. In Norse mythology, the Norns: Skuld, Verdandi, and Urd; weaving the fates of humanity into the shining tapestry of existence. Each thread that passed through their hands representing a human life—the knots and snarls and the tribulations of that soul.

On the Tangled Skein of Knot Work:

Designing the wheel is where a computer comes in handy. I can sketch one "slice" of the repeating knot-work design and scan that. I determine the angle of rotation for dividing up the circle by that number of pieces (in this case, seven repeating segments) and copy, rotate, and paste it digitally. Incongruities can be tweaked in a single segment to ensure that everything lines up correctly, and then copy/ rotate/paste. When the design is complete it is printed out, and I can transfer it by hand to the final painting surface.

It is amazing that monks used to accomplish this without digital aid. Without a computer it becomes a much more painstaking and meditative process.

Some of these discarded sketches found their concepts reused in the painting following the Wheel of Fortune: Justice. Lady Luck and Lady Justice are both blind. Luck turns her face aside and makes her decisions with what can seem to be arbitrary whim. Why does one man seem to move through life along a blessed path, while another man sits unnoticed at his feet holding up a begging bowl?

But Justice is purposeful and she sees through to truth with a piercing sight that belies her blindness. Her fairness is clear as she metes out her verdicts.

Justice

To the ancient Egyptians, when death claimed a soul, it was brought to be judged by the goddess Ma'at. She weighed the soul on her scales against a feather, and if found wanting, that soul was sent to the underworld.

There are those who say Justice is blind, but that is not so. Her eyes blaze white not with blindness, but the pure white of truth. She sees through mere flesh, peeling aside the layers of emotion, dissemination, illusion, and perception and into the heart where the unfettered awareness resides. There is no hiding. She stands for karma. The souls gathered in the butterflies hover near, and she bears the feather close to her heart like a sword.

She judges without her own bias or with grays of "maybes," but in terms of stark black and white. Things are as they are—fair, impartial, and right. And there is a balance that is achieved when true justice has been meted out. The scales are evened out and all is settled correctly.

MEANING

Balance, harmony, equilibrium, assuming responsibility, weighing all sides of an issue before making a decision, choosing with full awareness. Justice relies on a logical mind, capable of objective ruling on situations, and adjusting that which needs reassessment. Mediation on right, morality, and duty. Perhaps compromise must be made in order to truly even both sides of a situation. Admitting and acknowledging the truth. Comprehending the results of your actions and the connections they have to everything around. From that knowledge, setting a course for the future.

I toyed with the concept of giving her a Sword of Truth, but in the end could not work the blade into a satisfactory composition. Instead, the feather ended up playing the role of a double symbol: the feather of Ma'at to weigh on the scales, and as a sword blade brandished at her chest.

This initial version of Justice peered with far too much intensity and inquisitiveness at the soul (butterfly) for one who is blind and impartial. This was the sketch of a seeker, not a balancer. Nevertheless, I liked some of the motifs that presented themselves: the butterflies and the feather symbolically weighed upon her scales.

I also determined that Justice should be facing the viewer straight on, unwavering and sure. Turned aside like this she loses a great deal of her power and confidence.

The next version took up where the discarded Lady Luck sketches left off, further exploring the concepts that had first come to light there. The inverted wing was meant to represent her impartial weighing of both sides of what is presented.

On Butterflies:

Butterflies have long been symbols of the human soul. Perhaps the most well-known association is from the ancient Greek myth of Eros and Psyche (whose name means both butterfly and soul).

Psyche was a human maiden so beautiful that Eros, son of Aphrodite, fell in love with her. He knew this would madden his mother, so he spirited Psyche away in secret to be married. He took her to his palace, where she never glimpsed her husband but was waited on by invisible servants. At night under the cloak of darkness, her invisible husband came to her, and she grew to love him even never seeing his face.

Her sisters came to visit and were struck by jealousy for her obvious happiness, and they convinced Psyche that her mystery husband must be a monster afraid of the light. They played upon her fears. One night she waited until after Eros was asleep to light a candle and gaze upon his face. She was instantly struck by his beauty and realized it was no monster she was married to, but the god Eros! A drop of candle wax slipped from her trembling hand and fell upon his face. He shot awake and mournfully told her that now that she knew who he was he could not stay with her.

Left alone, Psyche then began the long process to regain the trust and love of Eros, working her way through the various trials that Aphrodite challenged her with.

sword of truth?

flock of butterfly-souls waiting to be weighed

12/8/06

Hanged Man

In the foggy depths of the woods, he dips his fingers into the red clay, and with a careful hand he trails the patterns across his skin. Across chest and arms and face. The spirals of red draw his mind into that place of deep meditation where thought becomes action, and where the stillness speaks with the voices of the gods.

When the silence in his soul is absolute, he rises to his feet. The spirits of the forest watch as he passes, in mute witness and respect. They reach out tentatively to touch his hallowed flesh and fall into his footsteps. With solemn dignity the procession arrives at the great Oak.

The Hanged Man makes his choice of self-sacrifice. He goes willingly to his fate, unhinges his grip on control, and endures for the sake of the rewards such knowing sacrifice may bring. Ivy creeps along his body binding and entwining him physically to the tree, until they are as one. Ivy: symbol of determination and the unbreakable strength and will of the human spirit.

In an echo of his action of faith and sacrifice, the fae fold back their wings and free fall from their perches in the tree, entrusting themselves to the winds.

MEANING

Letting go and surrendering to experience and emotional release. Accepting what is, and giving up control. Suspending action. Sacrifice. As Odin hung upon the World Tree Yggdrasil in his quest for knowledge, thus to attain the greatest rewards one must be willing to give up the self. The hanged man also urges you to reverse your view of the world and see things in a new light. Sometimes a change in one's perception of the world is required, a subtle shifting of the state of mind.

53

Hanged Man
FROM THE SKETCHBOOK

On Odin:

In Norse mythology, it is said that Odin sacrificed himself. For nine days and nights, he fasted as he hung upside-down from the branches of the great World Tree Yggdrasil. At the end of this time, he fell from the tree, having been enlightened by the secrets of runes. This knowledge, writing, was what he gifted to his mortal children.

It was this nature of sacrifice that I wished to encapsulate into the Hanged Man. One who goes to his fate, turning their world upside-down as it were, knowing that to achieve that which is most precious requires a yielding of the self.

Odin One-Eye
with Hugin & Mugin
Memory's Thought

hanging from
Yggdrassil for 9 days
5 nights seeking

Yggdrassil...
Sherwood Oak...
Elder trees...

Odin understands this concept. In addition to his trial upon Yggdrasil, for the sake of wisdom, intelligence, and foresight, he paid one eye for a drink from the enchanted Well of Mimir.

Random Tree Thoughts:

And what of the tree, which is as much as part of this image as the Hanged Man himself? Thoughts of Yggdrasil, a grand ash at whose roots is the Well of Mimir, whose branches spread across the heavens to cover the world; and of the Elder Oak of Sherwood Forest, a grand giant that truly exists, and in the hollow of which it is said the outlaws hid to be sheltered from their enemies.

The tumbling faery was a tribute to my artist friend James Browne, who gifted me a painting entitled "Faith" with a similar little one entrusting herself to the greater powers. The ultimate surrender: to close your eyes and fall back into the void, knowing that someone would guide the descent!

December 29 2004

On Ivy:

Ivy is tenacious, clinging and binding as it grows. Thus a symbol to the Druids of determination and strength.

Death

It is said that the mute swan is silent its entire life. Upon the threshold of death it sings one achingly beautiful song that steals the final breath from its chest; and then it expires upon that ultimate sigh. It is the most heartbreakingly wrenching song of ending.

But the song of the phoenix … ah, the song of the swan cannot compare.

When the phoenix sees death beckoning, she lifts her voice in a tragic song of pain, of rending, of sorrow … that yet cannot mask the most intense joy; for she knows that as the flames lick at her heart, the heat is quickening the egg in which her successor sleeps. Her deathflame is its lifespark. One is linked inextricably to the other. And thus she was tied to her predecessor, and she hers, and she hers, to the beginning of time. She sits in her deathbed, upon her nest, and she submits to the inevitable hand of fate. As the fire burns searing hot and white, she spreads her wings and breathes her final song of expiration.

MEANING

Closing the door to the past and opening a new one, going through transition, changing status, shedding the old and excess, bowing to inexorable forces and sweeping changes. The old must be set aside and burned away to make way for the new. The ancient story of the phoenix is one that is echoed and repeated in dozens of cultures. She is death and rebirth and life, encapsulated in a single symbol. Irises are associated with death, as Iris was the Greek goddess of the rainbow, which she used to travel down to Earth with messages from the gods and to transport women's souls to the underworld. Deadly nightshade is a highly poisonous plant—a symbol of deception, danger, and death.

And sumac, in the Victorian language of flowers, means "I shall survive the change."

Even before I ever con-
ceived of the idea of creating
this series of paintings, I always thought
of the Death card in tarot as a phoenix. The key
concept to emphasize being not Death as an ending, but
as a cleansing, a renewal, a necessary transition. It is not nightmare
phantom Death who hides in the shadows, skull-faced, wearing a black robe and bearing a scythe. Such a stereotype
was not conducive to the other subtleties of and layers of
meaning that this piece needed to encapsulate.

The phoenix is the perfect summary of the thoughts
I had. It is a blazing death, a beautiful transition;
a necessary component in the grand scheme
of the cycles of the world. The whole of it
was a reiteration of a concept that seemed to be
slowly threading its way through this entire series of
images: the interconnected web of all creation.

Iris. for Isis.

*Shape's a bit
like a butterfly,
...another kind
of death/metamor-
phosis/rebirth.*

On Flowers:

The language of flowers was a tradition that came into popularity during the Victorian era (though the concept was one rooted in antiquity), in which arrangements of different flowers and colors were used to convey messages.

The phoenix egg smolders like an ember. The next phoenix awaiting its chance to live when the old one self-immolates upon the nest. Fiery potential burning with a fierce intensity and a will to live.

Life tied to Death.

A dependent cycle.

"I will survive the change.

Temperance

She gathers herself. She reaches within for the calm center, that place of balance. From her center, she feels the dragon and phoenix stirring. They embrace in a sinuous twisting of scale and feather until it seems that one melts into the other. They coil around each other in a timeless battle for supremacy; choreographed in an elegant waltz of give and take, of push and pull. They swirl about her, in a maelstrom that assaults the senses. Like a maestro, she watches over and reins in one or the other when she senses any imbalance so that harmony is maintained.

Earth and sky, fire and water, male and female, the warmth and lush growth of summer and the chill winds of winter bearing down: these opposites flow one into the other in the cyclical and endless push of yin and yang. They are perfectly balanced against one another. In fact, they are given purpose and definition by the existence of their diametric opposite.

Without water, fire rages utterly unchecked and all-consuming, burning itself out eventually in a terrible conflagration. And without fire, the waters are lightless and drowning, flooding until there is only a still and silent mirror of nothing. By defining limits, they both are imbued with life and become life-giving: tempered to coexist with just the right balance, for too much of one and the other will be smothered.

MEANING

Harmony and equilibrium, balancing of opposites, healing. Moderation of extremes, self-restraint, harnessing absolute forces, and reining them in to be wielded to a purpose. Holding opposites apart from one another denies their power of unity. By drawing them together to merge in a measured fashion, and understanding what one bestows upon the other, a beautiful synthesis can be created. Sometimes all that holds the two apart is a wall of belief. Being flexible and understanding that there is more than one way to perceive the world can go a long way toward breaking down that invisible wall.

Temperance
FROM THE SKETCHBOOK

On the Dragon and Phoenix:

In China, the dragon and phoenix are the epitome of male (dragon) and female (phoenix) principles. Both of them are mythical entities, a fantastic melding of various creatures into one being. The phoenix possesses the beak of a rooster, the neck of a snake, the tail of a peacock, the legs of a crane. The dragon has the claws of an eagle, the body of a snake, the head of a lion, the crown of a stag. All these attributes are encapsulated by their singularly unique forms. Each in their way is a mirror of the concepts of Temperance.

The mingling of extreme opposites in a stable and balanced equilibrium. Not necessarily the mixture of two, for that would be a submerging of the identities and qualities of each.

The richness of black and the purity of white need not be turned into a meaningless neutral gray fog to achieve unity—rather, a careful integration of the two can create a beauty in pattern and flow. Like the balance of a carefully plotted black and white ink drawing. The purpose of Temperance is to maintain that which is unique while holding in check enough to coexist in balance.

Yin & yang.
phoenix - dragon
fire & water

Opposite Thoughts:

Juxtaposition of the spirit dragon and the phoenix with the more material ones of flesh and blood and stone. And within that pairing even, a contrast of cold marble against a living and breathing creature.

Devil

She feels the walls closing in on her. She is oblivious to the fact that she is not completely surrounded, that there is the wide world open to either side! The skies cry with songs of beauty and freedom. But she tucks her head down to hide in fear. Walls and shackles, though it is only a thin thread to bind her, red as her heart's blood; and the key is so close, so close.

Look up! You wish to cry at her. *Raise your eyes and look around!*

Her ears are deaf to any voice but that of the Devil. All she hears and feels is the Devil dancing above her, driving her, goading her, pressing down upon her. *Tap tap tap* goes the dancing of his hooves in a merry, mocking rhythm. *Tap tap tap* in the seductive patterns of entrapment of the willing. *Tap tap tap* he dances and he laughs with the knowledge that it is with such ease he can hold a vibrant spirit captive.

Look up! and faintly the voice pierces through the stones and seeps up into her body, and she reaches out.

MEANING

Losing independence, addiction and enslavement, caught up in the material, over-indulgence, choosing to stay in the dark. Over-indulging in pleasures, lust, and desire. Feeling hopelessness close in and limit the options. The Devil plays on your desires with a masterful touch. Break free from the puppeteer's strings, by looking beyond the material blockades and temptations.

The Devil has many faces. For this piece he did seem to wish to take on the form of a musician or a merry capering beast. Seductive in his rhythms, mesmerizing, enchanting. It is easy to deny an evil-faced demon; much harder not to fall victim to the trap that lulls the wariness and defenses, then creeps within like the thin and echoing strands of a song that will not leave the head.

You can see in this progression of sketches, he went from a more human proportioned creature, to something more otherworldly. He became drawn and angular, like a spider lurking in the dark recesses of the human heart.

Though these are visible incarnations of the Devil, in truth he is but the whispering weakness that everyone must overcome within themselves.

He weaves an intricate webwork around the human heart. He understands what beats in that precious ruby gem. He knows the deepest desires, the fears, the doubts. And understanding all of that, he can then architect a beautiful spider's web of lies, illusions, and half-truths to hold that heart in thrall.

Marionettes

On Marionettes:

The Devil is a master puppeteer. He manipulates the strings with such a slight and adept hand, like a stage magician, that these artifices of wood and twine appear fully lifelike, even perhaps imbued with the belief themselves that they are alive and real. From the puppet that he swings, a little soul reaches out, breaking free.

worn out.
dejected...
unwanted?
"oh woe is me!"

Tower

A seed drifts down on the wind, deposited lightly to the ground. From it a tree takes root. As the years turn, it grows—a slender sapling, glowing with green life.

And the years turn—grand and stately it reaches to the sky, challenges the heavens.

And the years turn—it is a mighty giant among giants, lovingly crafted living wood and greenery that is Nature's masterpiece.

Birds come to rest on its glorious limbs, joyous and full of songs inspired by the heat of the sun and the rush of the wind and the endless skies. Men and women come to sleep in its velvety dappled shade and dream visions of running water and soft dark loam and home. Even in the depths of winter, so thick and established has its network of branches and foliage become that there is shelter for any traveler, man or beast; a haven for any who should wearily pass by.

And the years turn—and it has been here forever, established and deep-rooted. Its branches touch the vault of the sky, brushing the stars lightly and caressing the moon as she swings past. Its roots reach into the earth to wrap around the pulsing beat that trembles in the darkness of the deeps.

And then with a fickle turn, as easily as she graced this tree with manifold blessings, Nature rescinds her gift. She throws a terrible spear from the heavens. What has taken centuries to coax forth from a tiny seed is destroyed in an instant in a deadly arc of blindingly beautiful blazing lightning.

It sunders.

It sears white hot.

It shatters to splinters. The earth shudders at the tremors of the blow.

MEANING

Catastrophe, sudden change, crisis, releasing all emotion, suffering a blow to the ego, revelation and seeing through illusions. A necessary disruption to the status quo; violent and explosive upheaval as the only way to break through the long-established patterns. Fantasies shattered by the harsh and brutal hand of reality. Making a clean and utter severing from the past. It is time to reexamine belief structures and opinions.

Tower
FROM THE SKETCHBOOK

On the Dragon's Spine:

I've always been drawn to the imagery of the Chinese feng shui lore that tells of the lands being perched along the backs of dragons. It sets such a fragile and precarious nature to the constructs of humans; that at any moment on the whim of Nature or of the whim of the dragon things could change. That by pure chance that deeply slumbering beast could shrug its shoulders in a dream. Or perhaps it would awaken with a mighty roar and a cascade of dirt and loam and houses. All that we create is but an itch along its spine with an illusion of security and stability. An interesting concept, although it did not make its way to the final sketch.

Various combinations of spires and towers sprang up in my sketchbook. But the final form was a city built in the treetops. Lightning rods spear upward from the branches, but it is not enough to deter the bolt that crackles through the dry air and strikes with the precision of a bolt from Zeus's fist, and with the painful randomness of Nature. In an instant, devastating fire, and this man-made construct of a tower that dares to defy the heavens comes tumbling down.

But we're a tenacious bunch, humans. However painful the catastrophe, it is never the end. What is destroyed gets built anew.

Stronger? Better? Perhaps. Different, most certainly, in its myriad ways.

"London bridge comes falling down,
falling down,
falling down.
London bridge
comes falling down,
my fair lady."

—A children's
nursery rhyme

Silver gilded footsteps
glide on silver flowing streams
with the silver glowing starlight
etching night in silver seams

Star

There is no sun. There is no moon. In the hushed stillness of the blackest night, only a trail of stars glitters like a fortune in diamonds upon the velvet carpet of the sky. The river of the Milky Way pours across the heavens in a cascade of starry pinpricks, and she comes dancing down that lane to where the celestial river runs to the silver etched earthly waters.

Water and earth and air become a single element in her presence. Walk on one, swim through the other, it matters not which; they are as she wills them to be.

She dances, and her feet are so light, there is but the barest disturbance of ripples upon her watery dance floor. She dances the dance that the stars have choreographed in their millennia of gazing down on the earth. It is their silent homage to the burning spirit they have witnessed. It is the dance and flow of human life, condensed into its pure essence of painful beauty. It is Hope made into a visual form.

She stretches and strains, sways and arches, leaps to impossible heights in time to a tempo that beats in the silent pulses of the stars above. A cascade of river droplets sprays forth from her swirling form. Where each droplet falls, a flowery tendril slowly sprouts.

She dances tirelessly through the night, inhuman, and yet embodying humanity in her very being. When the glow of dawn touches the eastern sky, she clasps her silvery cloak tight. There is a sudden weariness to her eyes, but it is edged with triumph as well. She steps up the slowly furling carpet of the Milky Way, back to her sister stars in the night, where they gleam and wait for the next true night to dance again.

MEANING

Regaining hope, faith in the future, inspiration. Finding the still and silent place within your being of serenity, tranquility amid trouble, harmony. Offering without reservations, sharing and being generous. The harshness of daylight or even moonlight is gone, and there is nothing but the calm and nonjudgmental eyes of the stars. There is a peace to that, a space to gather up, prepare, and uplift the spirit. Let loose doubts and fears to the embrace of the night. The stars have always been symbols of guidance and hope, the light to lead you home. Carp is a resilient fish that symbolizes strength, perseverance, courage, and determination of spirit. The chrysanthemums, commonly representative of longevity, are also symbols of hope.

Star

FROM THE SKETCHBOOK

"Star light, star bright,

First star I see tonight;

I wish I may, I wish I might

Have this wish I wish tonight."

—An English nursery rhyme

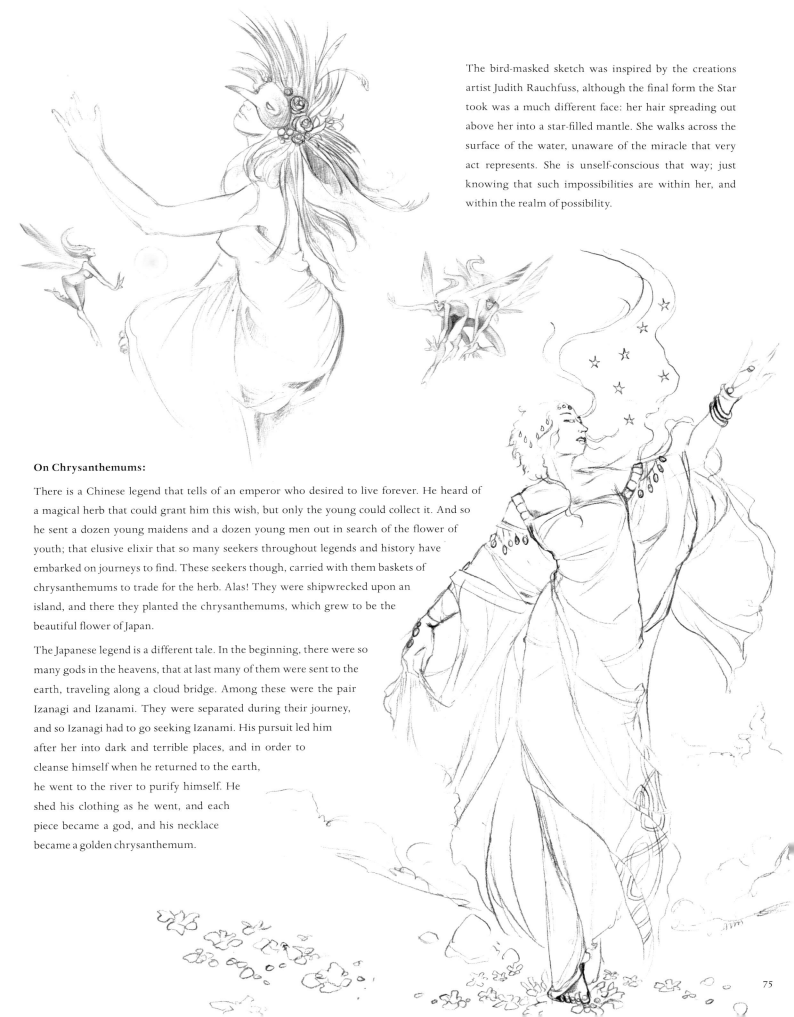

The bird-masked sketch was inspired by the creations artist Judith Rauchfuss, although the final form the Star took was a much different face: her hair spreading out above her into a star-filled mantle. She walks across the surface of the water, unaware of the miracle that very act represents. She is unself-conscious that way; just knowing that such impossibilities are within her, and within the realm of possibility.

On Chrysanthemums:

There is a Chinese legend that tells of an emperor who desired to live forever. He heard of a magical herb that could grant him this wish, but only the young could collect it. And so he sent a dozen young maidens and a dozen young men out in search of the flower of youth; that elusive elixir that so many seekers throughout legends and history have embarked on journeys to find. These seekers though, carried with them baskets of chrysanthemums to trade for the herb. Alas! They were shipwrecked upon an island, and there they planted the chrysanthemums, which grew to be the beautiful flower of Japan.

The Japanese legend is a different tale. In the beginning, there were so many gods in the heavens, that at last many of them were sent to the earth, traveling along a cloud bridge. Among these were the pair Izanagi and Izanami. They were separated during their journey, and so Izanagi had to go seeking Izanami. His pursuit led him after her into dark and terrible places, and in order to cleanse himself when he returned to the earth, he went to the river to purify himself. He shed his clothing as he went, and each piece became a god, and his necklace became a golden chrysanthemum.

You demi-puppets that
By moonshine do the green sour ringlets make,
Whereof ewe not bites; and you, whose pastime
Is to make midnight mushrooms …

—Shakespeare, *The Tempest* (act V, scene 1)

Moon

The watchful eye of the sun has closed, and the harshness that day shines upon the world is blurred and erased. The moon rises upon this, her domain, to spy on those of the half-world who begin to creep forth. A mushroom faery ring glows bright in those soft silvery waves. As the moments pass and the gloam closes in, they glow brighter and brighter with their own phosphorescence to light the path for the faery queen. *"She comes hither!"* cry the sprites on the wind, with voices so lovely they drive mortals mad with longing. *"Make way!"* call the will-o'-the-wisps, darting through the woods. They spark and glitter to taunt and lead astray any human who might be passing, but there is no human toy for them to catch ahold of tonight. The dryads clasp hands from among the gray birches and shed their leaves as they step forward lightly as handmaids to the approaching queen. As she glides through the forest, anemones spring up beneath her bare feet, and she smiles as she begins the dancing.

Make way! Make way!
The night holds sway;
lead on the dance to fend off day!
With mad delight come hear us sing:
no sorrow here, no ponderous thought,
no secrets held, no secrets sought,
for all that's wrought in faery's ring
is wild abandon.
Let sense take wing!

MEANING

Fears and anxieties, believing illusions, experiencing distortion and chasing after fantasy, dreams and visions, disorientation. The fae are masterful at the arts of illusion, and the dangers of stepping into a mushroom faery ring are well known. The Moon is the realm beyond the known and comforting and predictable. It is the otherworld, awesome and inspiring in its own right, and daunting and dangerous if ill-respected. It is easy to be the wayward traveler who is distracted by will-o'-the-wisps and led astray to be lost wandering in the woods; but if one keeps the wits about, a glimpse beyond the bounds of sunlit reality is the rarest honor and most inspiring of enchantments. It is a doorway to hidden unknowns, and the wellspring of mingled dark and light that seeps forth from there.

That is the gift of the Moon.

It is said that to be touched by the moon's rays in slumber is to court lunacy. I look up at the moon on a still night, and feel that spiderweb trailing of silver light across my face. No heat like the caress of the sun. No sign of that ghostly trailing of light except what my imagination fills. A peace steals across the room, the stillness of meditation, of delving down within.

Cast off the masks, the faces for the daylight. Second skins. This face is for happiness. This face is for responsibility. This for necessity, for presentation, for expectation.

One by one, set the masks aside, like sentimental necklaces tucked into a jewelry box, each one a present gifted by a time, a person, a place, a need. Remembered and hoarded. Until suddenly the box is overflowing. The garnets glitter seductively, the jade beckons with a mossy caress of comfort.

In the moonlight that pierces through the window, they suddenly look like plastic and glass nestled in the velvet.

Which face was real? A bare face is a forgotten sensation now. Naked and vulnerable.

Turn aside, move to the silvered panes. Tilt the face up to bathe in that primal light of the moon, to let the silver fingers trail across brow and nose and lip. More delicate than a cobweb. More intimate than the touch of the dearest lover. She lays a silver mask with her silver threads. The only mask that matters.

Open the eyes. It's invisible in the night. It melts in the sunlight, and leaves in its wake freedom.

On Mushroom Rings:

Folktales say that mushrooms growing in a circle mark the enchanted places where faeries danced the night before. Faery revels are a danger to humans, for the folk of the otherworld know no human limits, and an eternity of real time can pass in what may seem a single drunken night.

Cats:
Nocturnal fuzzballs
of chaos

Sun

In a flare of liquid gold that pours across the sky, the sun rises. It is the brilliant star of day, banishing the thin and wispy light of his night-bound siblings in the rich glow of dawn.

As the morning mist rises in hazy waves from the dew-dampened ground, the King of the Birds emerges from his slumbering roost. His feathers gleam iridescent under dawn's rosy palette of warmth-tinged light. His companion mounts and together they set wing across the lands of their domain. They glide across the valleys, hearing the songs rise from workers in the fields. They soar up high and taunt the mountaintops with an elusive brush of wingtips across the upper peaks.

The denizens of the day come to trail in an entourage of avian delight. They pour across the sky, trailing after the sun in the arc of its journey to the western horizon.

> *From fallow field and verdant vale,*
> *from sun-bleached shores with diamond grains,*
> *and moonlit trails that trek like veins*
> *through mountain, river; past the end*
> *where sky is but a ghostly veil*
> *That to Beyond transcends …*
>
> *I summon all the winged kin*
> *From this horizon to the bounds*
> *Of what is dreamt and all surrounds!*
> *The voices of forbidden songs*
> *Will spiral through and center in*
> *To fall where they belong!*

MEANING

Enlightenment and understanding, glory, achieving prominence. The constant renewal of life and vitality. Being filled with radiant joy and energy, invigoration, and good health. Being full of assurance and confidence, a clarity of vision and purpose lit by the clear daylight. From the times of ancient civilizations up to the present, the sun has always been a symbol of life and growth. It has been embodied in vibrant gods and goddesses in cultures throughout the ages—young and glorious and brilliant, full of vigor, and blazing splendor. The strength and power of the gods pours forth in the nourishing glow of the sun.

Sun
FROM THE SKETCHBOOK

I walk along a dark path in a dream.

Sidewalks edged by the crashing sea. It is a strange juxtaposition. The glint of no light on sea spray is the only illumination. But there is no scent, either. There is no wetness amidst the turbulence. It is curiously silent.

In the burn of morning light, the mists peel back from the ground. The last stray tendrils evaporate in the golden haze of sunlight as if physical fingers reach out to brush away the tenaciously clinging cobwebs.

That strange pathway is a half-forgotten vision within the first few moments of the glimmering day; so distant, a world away. The sun beckons from beyond the slated blinds, with the myriad voices of the birds, in a dozen notes, in a hundred singing dust motes.

Let illusions fall away beneath this brilliance!

As a king of the skies, he needed a winged companion. To complete the full array for his escort, and to fill the page with the color and light and life that is the sun: the sparrows, hawks, jays, crows, geese. In a position of honor, a little red-breasted hummingbird, symbolic that the smallest is not necessarily the least, as well as being a little tribute to the creatures who visit my window in the summer months, drawn to the rosebush in the courtyard garden.

No ordinary steed, or even a horse is his mount.

He rides on a peacock-like bird, with brilliant plumage, and proud crown. A king among the avian creatures.

Judgment

Upon the arrival of Judgment Day, an angel sounds the horn to send out the Blast of Truth. Let all the souls rise to that call then and lay their deeds out to be seen and judged by all. Let the spirit be cleansed with burning light and fire, to be made pure. There comes a time for everyone when an accounting must be held. It is time to evaluate the phase of life just past, to recognize and to honestly appraise with an unbiased mind. Honesty to oneself. Every action has its result, for good or for ill, to be rewarded or to bear the need for absolution and forgiveness, cleansing and atonement. And beyond that is the transition on to the next phase, a rebirth and a clean slate to begin again.

Red poppies are a symbol of sleep and death, sometimes as an offering for the dead. Like blood, their color stains the fields, brilliant and beautiful. From that life-filled expanse of delicately swaying crimson and gold, butterflies take wing to bear the spirits onward in the metamorphosis of the soul. The wide freedom, and the endless blue of the beyond awaits.

MEANING

Release and renewal, absolution, the freshness of a new dawn, a new start. Making a judgment, though it might be harsh and difficult to face; the necessity of hard choices. Face down those decisions, recognize the need, and forgive. Reawakening, the mystery of birth and death. The voice of destiny summons you onward. Hearing that undeniable call, and being drawn to act upon it; knowing what must be done.

On Poppies:

Poppies are often symbols for sleep and oblivion, because of the narcotic (opium) that is extracted from them, and death for the blood red color of some varieties—said to be sprung from Christ's blood on his journey to Golgotha. They are often etched on tombstones as an emblem of the eternal sleep. The Roman god of sleep, Somnus, was often depicted wearing a crown woven of poppies, and it was said that Demeter, goddess of the harvest, created poppies to grant herself the peace of slumber when she lost her daughter Persephone to the underworld of Hades.

There is a strange contrast of all that sleep and death symbology with the simple beauty and enchantment of a field of poppies swaying in the breeze on a warm spring day. And because this piece is not about death, but renewal and the fresh start, I chose not the crimson color of death, but a golden orange color of hope. Which, incidentally, is also the color of my lovely local California poppies and so a personal touch.

From this sunlit field of golden poppies rise the cleansed souls. They are pulled upward into that terrifying and beautiful empty blue sky. What lies beyond the clear vault of the heavens?

On Butterflies:

Once again in the role they have played throughout this series of paintings, the butterflies are symbolic of the soul.

World

The pulse of the World ripples in an affirmation of all the life that it holds, and all the death that passes. Every leaf and tree, every creature from the smallest insects to the great singing whales, the patterns that they weave as they are born and die and cycle onward—they all tremble in unison with that single heartbeat, brought together by a mighty conductor. It is a wonderfully discordant harmony, the essence of balance, and a unity of such disparate parts.

She sets the crown of insight lightly on her brow. She wears the girdle of truth. She reaches within, and feels the lifeline that she is connected to as well. She touches it, and it is like a tangible presence in her heart, delicate but strong. The shining web of connections stretches from her heart and out into the nether. And then she reaches out with her mind, above, so high! She feels at one with the soaring birds, knows the stretch and strain of wing muscles flexing and balancing on the wind, knows the kiss of sunlight on her outstretched leaves and branches, feels the slow erosion of water on stone over the millennia.

There is no past or present or later, for this heartbeat has pulsed from the first spark of the universe, and it will beat until the end of time. It is an everlasting moment of now, and the shimmering web of connection thrums gloriously hot in her veins. With a sudden clarity, she knows in that instant that she is blessed.

MEANING

Satisfaction and peace of mind. A successful conclusion, and the end is in sight. Achieving balance, melding and blending to bring together in unison the multiple songs of life. The World is a card of realized goals and prosperity. It is a state of completion, though not without a share of involvement and hard work to attain. When one's goals have been reached, there is a space, a quiet breath of a moment in time when a feeling of ultimate fulfillment spills through the consciousness. It is a wondrous and precious moment, the culmination of hard work to see your dreams come true, and to know that elusively mythical treasure promised in fairy tales: the Heart's Desire.

World
FROM THE SKETCHBOOK

She began inhuman, but slowly those otherworldly aspects fell away because she needed to be mortal. Not angelic, not of the faery realms. Her knowledge is not only the providence of the divine. In fact, mortality is a key component of that interwoven reality.

It is the measure by which we can appreciate that which is fleeting. She is mortal in order to attain that connection with all that lives and breathes and dies, and the whole of the fragile yet beautiful World.

That which is eternal is forever separated from the rest of creation. But that which lives and dies becomes a part of it all.

Eternal.

The orb clutched to her abdomen felt too maternal.
Clutched close to her brow it becomes intellectual instead,
like a kind of communion and transfer of understanding.

The dispersion of sacred knowledge.

Cycles

No beginnings.

No ends.

The woven cycle of connection.